MIRACLES

12 Studies for Individuals or Groups

ROBBIE CASTLEMAN

Harold Shaw Publishers • Wheaton, Illinois

For my sister Kellie

ISBN 0-87788-555-9

Cover photo © by P. E. Sgrignoli

02 01 00 99 98 97 96

10 9 8 7 6 5 4 3 2 1

CONTENTS

INTRODUCTION

Miracles are unpredictable. I remember praying fervently for miraculous healing for my seven-year-old son who suffered from asthma. Our church elders were called, he was anointed with oil, and we believed that God *could* heal. We affirmed that our good Father is not the author of disease, but the Overcomer of all the consequences of sin in our world. There was no change in his condition. Over the years, Robert has "outgrown" his asthma like many other believing and unbelieving people. Sometimes miracles don't happen.

I also remember praying less fervently and with much more ambivalence for my own healing several years ago. The specialist had found "four very old and possibly pre-cancerous nodes" on my vocal cords. Surgery was imperative. I wanted to accept this trial with real faith—to trust God with a lengthy time of post-surgical silence. I had an inkling it might even be good for my soul, . . . I talk too much! But I also believed God could miraculously heal me if he knew this to be his best for me. I prayed about how to pray, how to trust, and how to rest in God's perfect will. I didn't pray "fervently." I didn't call the elders. I wasn't anointed with oil. A few students at a Bible study I taught prayed for me. And when I went for my pre-operative visit, the doctor was astounded: "I've never seen nodes this large and this old just disappear. Not a trace." I could hardly believe it either. I hadn't really sought healing. Sometimes miracles do happen.

It's hard to understand how faith, prayer, miracles, and the sovereign will of God all fit together. In my life and in the Old and New Testaments, miracles seem to be connected *to* faith but are not *dependent* on faith. In the book of Acts, chapter 12, the young Christian church prayed fervently and faithfully for intervention, and still the apostle James was beheaded. In the same chapter, after James's death, the church prayed fervently but fearfully for Peter's safety, and he was miraculously led out of prison by an angel. If miracles were dependent solely on the amount of faith exercised by praying people, James would have been set free too. It is clear that our exercise of faith does not dictate the will of God. Miracles are not the products of a vending-machine God, produced automatically when believers have put in the right amount of faith and pushed the right button.

Depending on how you count the miracles of Jesus, there are less than twenty-five total accounts, including times when more than one person was healed. In his book, *The Jesus I Never Knew,* Philip Yancey reflects on the unpredictability of the miracles of Jesus: "The healings were diverse and fit no real pattern. At least one person Jesus healed long-distance; some were instant and some gradual; many required the healed person to follow specific instructions." Though there was no pattern, still Jesus seemed to be strategic with his miracles. There was a purpose beyond simply restoring someone's withered hand or sight, which would be lost to death eventually. Hebrews 2:3-4 tells us that miracles were one way the truth of salvation was confirmed: "This salvation, which was first announced by the Lord, was confirmed to us by those who heard him. God also testified to it by signs, wonders and various miracles, and gifts of the Holy Spirit distributed according to his will."

Jesus urged his disciples to believe in him "on the evidence of the miracles themselves" (John 14:11). However, Jesus refused to "prove" himself by the miraculous to those around him who sought signs as proof of his authority—the familiar and yet faithless people of Nazareth, the thief on the cross, those who would make him king in order to get more "loaves and fishes," Pontius Pilate, and others. "A wicked and adulterous generation asks for a miraculous sign!" he warned. Yet miracles were and are signs that point us to Jesus, the Son of God. To believe in the Miracle Maker is the purpose of the miracle (John 20:30-31).

Miracles in Scripture reveal a God who indwells history immanently. There are miracles of healing, protection, provision, guidance, and nature in both the Old and New Testaments. God breaks into time and space for his own purposes and glory to remind us of a greater reality beyond our senses and expectations.

So how are we to think about miracles in this scientific age? Are we to seek them? Are miracles dependent on our show of faith? Is God still doing miracles today? This studyguide looks at a few miracles in the Bible, which will give us a glimpse into the heart of God, his will for the world, and his love for all creation. As Christians we are to live "by faith, not by sight" (2 Cor. 5:7). Faith-filled people can be surprised by what they see, and at times, surprised by what they don't see. It is my hope that this study of miracles will help this generation of God's people *see* the Savior, and not *seek* the sign. And that we will be ready for both at any time.

HOW TO USE THIS STUDYGUIDE

Fisherman studyguides are based on the inductive approach to Bible study. Inductive study is discovery study; we discover what the Bible says as we ask questions about its content and search for answers. This is quite different from the process in which a teacher *tells* a group *about* the Bible and what it means and what to do about it. In inductive study God speaks directly to each of us through his Word.

A group functions best when a leader keeps the discussion on target, but this leader is neither the teacher nor the "answer person." A leader's responsibility is to *ask*—not *tell*. The answers come from the text itself as group members examine, discuss, and think together about the passage.

There are four kinds of questions in each study. The first is an *approach question*. Used before the Bible passage is read, this question breaks the ice and helps you focus on the topic of the Bible study. It begins to reveal where thoughts and feelings need to be transformed by Scripture.

Some of the earlier questions in each study are *observation questions* designed to help you find out basic facts—who, what, where, when, and how.

When you know what the Bible says you need to ask, *What does it mean?* These *interpretation questions* help you to discover the writer's basic message.

Application questions ask, *What does it mean to me?* They challenge you to live out the Scripture's life-transforming message.

Fisherman studyguides provide spaces between questions for jotting down responses and related questions you would like to raise in the group. Each group member should have a copy of the studyguide and may take a turn in leading the group.

A group should use any accurate, modern translation of the Bible such as the *New International Version,* the *New American Standard Bible,* the *Revised Standard Version,* the *New Jerusalem Bible,* or the *Good News Bible.* (Other translations or paraphrases of the Bible may be referred to when additional help is needed.) Bible commentaries should not be brought to a Bible study because they tend to dampen discussion and keep people from thinking for themselves.

SUGGESTIONS FOR GROUP LEADERS

1. Read and study the Bible passage thoroughly beforehand, grasping its themes and applying its teachings for yourself. Pray that the Holy Spirit will "guide you into truth" so that your leadership will guide others.

2. If the studyguide's questions ever seem ambiguous or unnatural to you, rephrase them, feeling free to add others that seem necessary to bring out the meaning of a verse.

3. Begin (and end) the study promptly. Start by asking someone to pray for God's help. Remember, the Holy Spirit is the teacher, not you!

4. Ask for volunteers to read the passages out loud.

5. As you ask the studyguide's questions in sequence, encourage everyone to participate in the discussion. If some are silent, ask, "What do you think, Heather?" or, "Dan, what can you add to that answer?" or suggest, "Let's have an answer from someone who hasn't spoken up yet."

6. If a question comes up that you can't answer, don't be afraid to admit that you're baffled! Assign the topic as a research project for someone to report on next week.

7. Keep the discussion moving and focused. Though tangents will inevitably be introduced, you can bring the discussion back to the topic at hand. Learn to pace the discussion so that you finish a study each session you meet.

8. Don't be afraid of silences: some questions take time to answer and some people need time to gather courage to speak. If silence persists, rephrase your question, but resist the temptation to answer it yourself.

9. If someone comes up with an answer that is clearly illogical or unbiblical, ask him or her for further clarification: "What verse suggests that to you?"

10. Discourage Bible-hopping and overuse of cross-references. Learn all you can from *this* passage, along with a few important references suggested in the studyguide.

11. Some questions are marked with a ♦. This indicates that further information is available in the Leader's Notes at the back of the guide.

12. For further information on getting a new Bible study group started and keeping it functioning effectively, read Gladys Hunt's *You Can Start a Bible Study Group* and *Pilgrims in Progress: Growing through Groups* by Jim and Carol Plueddemann.

SUGGESTIONS FOR GROUP MEMBERS

1. Learn and apply the following ground rules for effective Bible study. (If new members join the group later, review these guidelines with the whole group.)

2. Remember that your goal is to learn all that you can *from the Bible passage being studied.* Let it speak for itself without using Bible commentaries or other Bible passages. There is more than enough in each assigned passage to keep your group productively occupied for one session. Sticking to the passage saves the group from insecurity and confusion.

3. Avoid the temptation to bring up those fascinating tangents that don't really grow out of the passage you are discussing. If the topic is of common interest, you can bring it up later in informal conversation following the study. Meanwhile, help each other stick to the subject!

4. Encourage each other to participate. People remember best what they discover and verbalize for themselves. Some people are naturally shyer than others, or they may be afraid of making a mistake. If your discussion is free and friendly and you show real interest in what other group members think and feel, they will be more likely to speak up. Remember, the more people involved in a discussion, the richer it will be.

5. Guard yourself from answering too many questions or talking too much. Give others a chance to express themselves. If you are one who participates easily, discipline yourself by counting to ten before you open your mouth!

6. Make personal, honest applications and commit yourself to letting God's Word change you.

MIRACLES AND THE MIRACLE WORKER

Exodus 17:1-7; Numbers 20:2-13

Comedian Robin Williams has commented: "Our kids embody our greatest fantasies and our worst nightmares. On one hand, I see my kid standing before the cameras saying, 'I'd like to thank the Nobel Committee.' On the other hand, I see him saying, 'You want ketchup with those?'" I catch myself in a similar double-minded dilemma when it comes to my walk with God. I can be a trusting child one minute and the next I'm trying to be an independent and inconsistent adolescent. Does my imperfect faith affect God's miraculous work? Sometimes when I've been least faithful in my ministry—had a lousy attitude, lacked prayer, and done things in my own strength—still God blessed people. Other times when I've prayed like crazy and depended fully on the Lord, people didn't even show up and ministry seemed fruitless.

We are all saints and sinners at once. We take valiant steps of faith, and we blow it. Moses and the tribes of Israel, wandering between Egypt and the Promised Land, knew what it was to be blessed as imperfect and sinful people. They knew what it was like to suffer with thirst even when they were doing their best to obey. And miracles happened during both extremes of their inconsistency. God is always faithful, even when he is unpredictable.

1. Relate a time in your experience when you have been blessed despite a sinful attitude. Or, share a time when you have been prayerful and obedient and the outcome was disappointing.

Read Exodus 17:1-7.

2. How were the people of Israel obedient to the Lord? How were they sinful?

3. How did Moses interpret their conduct (verse 2)?

4. How was faith both lacking and evident in the people? How was faith both lacking and evident in Moses (verse 4)?

5. How did God respond to Moses' prayer?

♦ **6.** Describe the miracle that took place.

Given Moses' fear (verse 4), why might initial obedience to God's command have been difficult for him?

7. How did this miracle address the question of the people reflected in verse 7?

Read Numbers 20:2-13.

♦ **8.** How was the complaint of the people similar to the earlier episode in Exodus? How was it different?

♦ *Indicates further information in Leader's Notes*

♦ **9.** What changes were evident in Moses' attitude toward the people in these two situations?

10. What did the Lord command Moses to do this time? What did Moses do?

♦ **11.** Why did God discipline Moses and Aaron (verse 12)?

How does Scripture summarize God's greatest concern (verses 12-13)?

12. In his grace, God miraculously provided a grumbling people with water in spite of the disobedience and sinful attitude of their leader. How have you seen this dynamic at work today in the church? in your life? Discuss.

13. What keeps you from trusting that God can miraculously meet your needs? How can you be more aware of God's holiness and grace?

MIRACLES AND OBEDIENCE

Jonah 1:1-17; 3:1–4:11

During my junior year in college I attended my first small group Bible study. It was a Friday night in April, and I wanted to be gone from my room so my phone would ring and ring, in case the guy who had just broken up with me decided to call. I wanted to meet another nice guy to date. I was bored, lonely, and didn't have any other invitations. These were the only reasons I went.

I am eternally grateful that the grace of God is not limited to people with good motives. God had a completely different reason for me being there that Friday night! It was the first night I clearly heard the gospel and my heart began to open to the love of the Savior. God desires our motives to be rightly aligned with his will. He had to get the prophet Jonah's attention in some drastic ways and worked miracles in spite of Jonah's poor attitude. But as we will see from Jonah's story, when it comes to people's salvation, God's miracles don't always depend on our obedience.

1. When has God worked through you to bless others despite a less-than-perfect attitude or motive on your part? Or when have you been blessed despite the sinfulness of another?

Read Jonah 1:1-17.

♦ **2.** Why was Jonah on the run?

♦ **3.** How did Jonah describe himself to the sailors? (Consider both verses 9 and 10.)

How do you think Jonah might have felt when the captain asked him to pray and the sailors confronted him?

4. What miracle did God provide to rescue Jonah and spare the ship? How was the storm itself a part of the miracle?

5. What was the result of God's miraculous display of power (verses 15-16)?

Jonah had three days and three nights inside a large fish to rethink his position and remember who God was. The fish then vomited Jonah onto dry land.

Read Jonah 3:1-10.

6. The Ninevites very possibly had heard of Jonah's amazing miraculous deliverance. How might this knowledge have heightened their attention to his message?

7. What miracles do you find happening in this chapter? How does it differ from the miracles in chapter 1?

8. Have you experienced this miracle of belief and repentance in your own life, or seen it clearly in anyone else's life? If so, what changes has God brought about?

Read Jonah 4:1-11.

9. Compare the conversations between Jonah and God in verses 3-4 and verses 8-9. Why was Jonah upset each time?

10. How might God's straightforward questions in verses 4 and 9 have helped Jonah evaluate his motives and feelings?

11. What sort of miracles did God use in this chapter to instruct his prophet?

◆ **12.** How did God summarize his motives and mercy for Nineveh in verses 10-11? In what way had God displayed the same mercy for Jonah?

13. God's desire to bring salvation was not tempered by the selfish motives and sinful attitude of his servant Jonah. In what way is a person's salvation the ultimate miracle?

Discuss ways you've seen God's salvation offered to others even today through imperfect Christians or imperfect situations.

MIRACLES AND FAITHFULNESS

Daniel 1:1-16; 3:1-27

Children often declare sincere but unrealistic oaths to back up their promises: "I promise. Cross my heart and hope to die!" Similarly, my high school yearbook contains numerous promises to be "friends forever"—from people I have never seen again. A verbal oath or sincere feelings do not guarantee that promises will be kept. Anyone who is married knows that it's the *staying* married, not the sweetest of romantic sentiments, that validates the wedding vows. And it's the same with our faith. Following through in obedience is its own oath.

But what do we do when staying faithful to God puts us in situations that are overwhelmingly costly or difficult? As four men in ancient Babylon discovered, our unwillingness to compromise may bring us to a point where a miracle becomes necessary for fidelity or even survival. When we commit ourselves faithfully to God, we will find him miraculously there with us.

1. Think of a time in your life or someone else's in which faithfulness to God led to inconvenience or hardship, and which resulted in the miraculous intervention of God. How did you (or they) respond to the difficulty?

Read Daniel 1:1-16.

♦ **2.** What efforts were made to immerse these four men from Judah in the Babylonian culture?

♦ **3.** What did Daniel do to demonstrate his unwillingness to compromise his commitment and obedience to Yahweh, the Lord? Who joined Daniel in this resistance?

4. What was the first indication that God was miraculously at work to protect and prosper Daniel and his friends?

How did the honesty of the court official in verse 10 influence the impact of the miracle to unbelievers?

5. How did Daniel's proposal to the official reflect his faith in God and make the miraculous work of God essential?

Read Daniel 3:1-27.

6. What was the situation King Nebuchadnezzar created to elevate himself above all the gods of the nations and peoples he conquered?

What "idols" today tempt us to deny God his supreme place in our lives?

7. How might Nebuchadnezzar's reaction to the resistance of the Jews make their faithfulness to the true God especially challenging?

8. Judging from their reply to Nebuchadnezzar's threat (verses 16-18), do you think Shadrach, Meshach, and Abednego were confident in God's protection? Why or why not?

9. Describe the miraculous protection and deliverance of these Jewish men. How do the details help you visualize and believe this narrative?

10. How did God manifest his presence in this miracle, both to the faithful believers and to the pagan king (verses 24-25)?

11. In what ways are you tempted today to compromise godly values and your promise of faithfulness to God?

Is depending on the miraculous work of God difficult for you in these situations? Why or why not?

MIRACLES AND POWER

John 6:1-15, 25-35

My father-in-law is well remembered by the people in the church he pastored for thirty years. After his reluctant retirement at the age of seventy, a leader in the church commented that it would be "hard to replace a pastor who routinely helped take out the garbage after a church pot-luck dinner." He was right. Talented or powerful people are actually more "replaceable" than the truly humble leaders.

Those with the ability and opportunity to meet the needs of others (for example, pastors, counselors, politicians, and kings) often face the temptation to use their good works and benevolence to gain power and position for themselves. "Miracle workers" can encourage the prestige that leads to pride and the possible misuse of power. Jesus certainly had miraculous abilities and opportunities to impress people and meet their needs. But he avoided the temptation to perform "on demand" by taking deliberate steps to do miracles only for the purposes of God's kingdom.

1. Can you identify an area of talent, spiritual strength or giftedness that others appreciate in you, but which also tempts you to use it for prideful gain or personal advancement? How have you handled it?

Read John 6:1-15.

♦ **2.** Why were the people so eager to find Jesus?

What would be enticing about having crowds of people want your services? What would be difficult about this?

3. How did Jesus respond to the converging crowd?

4. What reason did Jesus express for gathering up the bread?

Why do you think Jesus asked the *disciples* in particular to gather the leftovers?

♦ **5.** Considering the mindset and nature of the crowd, what other reason might Jesus' have had for the careful accounting of the leftovers? (How might it have been used or abused by the people?)

How can Christians avoid making a truly supernatural work into mere superstition?

♦ **6.** Note the crowd's response to this miracle (verses 14-15). Why did Jesus withdraw from the crowd?

What does this show us about his understanding of people's attraction to power?

Read John 6:25-35.

7. After recrossing the Sea of Galilee, the people still pursued Jesus. How did Jesus summarize their motives?

♦ **8.** What did the people actually want from Jesus at this time (verses 28, 30-31)?

Do you think the people fully understood this miracle (verse 34)? Why or why not?

9. In contrast to barley loaves and fish, what kind of food did Jesus want the people to desire?

How can earthly, physical desires dull our appetites for spiritual "food"?

10. How did Jesus summarize the "work" God desires for those who follow him?

11. Contrast the people's use of the verb "do" with Jesus' use of the verb "believe" (verses 28-29). Which verb is the stronger motivation in your own faith?

How does this motivation relate to or affect how you view miracles?

12. Jesus identified himself as the One to whom this "miraculous sign" pointed. How is Jesus himself, as the Bread of Life, the ultimate miracle in your life?

MIRACLES AND MERCY

Matthew 14:22-33

During the 1960s, many young people who came to believe in Christ were known as "Jesus Freaks." I was one of them. Our youthful enthusiasm gave us a pretty radical faith. We shared our food extravagantly, gave away clothes, and studied the Bible for hours. In our "church in the park" we prayed fervently for people to be delivered from drug addiction or for grocery money to be provided, and we saw miracles happen before our eyes. These gifts of grace were very evident to us. We also did some pretty stupid things that hurt us and others. Through all of this God was faithful and steadfast. In his mercy he rescued us from situations caused by foolish enthusiasm and rebuked us for acts of willfulness that threatened our faith.

"Miracles are but parables of prayer" wrote E.M. Bounds in his book, *The Reality of Prayer.* Both miracles (God's part) and prayer (our part) are startling reminders that the Eternal invades time, the Creator still touches creation, and a Holy God still loves unholy people. In prayer, our Father listens to our cries; in miracle, our Father acts on our behalf to reveal himself to us and provide for our needs. Both rescue and rebuke can be part of God's purpose for working a miracle. The apostle Peter discovered this firsthand in a remarkable experience with Jesus.

♦ **1.** How do prayer and miracles show us God's grace? His mercy?

Read Matthew 14:22-33.

2. What miracle of provision had Jesus just performed before dismissing the crowd (see verses 19-21)?

3. What might have been some of Jesus' concerns during his time of prayer?

4. When Jesus went to the disciples on the lake, it was the "fourth watch of the night"—between 3:00 and 6:00 A.M. When had Jesus begun praying (verse 23)?

What does that indicate to you about his commitment to prayer?

5. How did the disciples first react when they saw Jesus walking on the lake?

What do you learn about Jesus from his response to them?

6. Why do you think Peter wanted to walk to Jesus on the water?

What might he have been feeling or thinking as he left the boat?

◆ **7.** Why do you think Jesus encouraged Peter to "come" to him on the water?

8. Peter cried out a short and desperate prayer to Jesus. How does a life-threatening crisis affect your efforts and energy in prayer? Are you less confident or more confident in God during these times? Why?

9. Why was Jesus' rebuke important for Peter and the others?

10. Note the disciples' response in verse 33. Why do you think these events resulted in this recognition?

How did the combination of miracle and humanity contribute to this insight?

11. What examples in this story do you see of these pairs: prayer and miracle, faith and failure, rescue and rebuke, fear and worship?

How is worship of God a proper response to the side-by-side reality of miracle and humanity in our lives?

12. If you had been with the disciples on this night, would you have wanted to join Peter? Why or why not?

13. How does this story influence your understanding of miracles? of prayer? of grace and mercy?

MIRACLES AND PRAYER

Mark 9:14-29

"Let go and let God" is a popular slogan found on key chains, wall plaques, desk accessories, and church banners. "Let go and let God" is the sincere advice of relatives and friends who feel *you* need to have faith in a difficult situation. "Let go and let God" work miracles in our lives and others' lives is easy to say, often harder to hear, and always impossible to do—without prayer.

Without prayer, this phrase is only a religious platitude. Without prayer, the believer never really "lets go." Without prayer, we aren't serious about "letting God." Prayer demonstrates our humble dependence on God. Prayer allows us to join in on what God is doing. Jesus taught and demonstrated that prayer is imperative if the power of God is to be seen in the miraculous.

1. When has prayer helped you prepare for a special work of God in your life?

Read Mark 9:14-29.

2. What groups make up the scene here when Jesus arrives? What are they arguing about?

◆ **3.** Look back at Mark 9:2-7. What had Jesus experienced just prior to this encounter?

How might Jesus' experience on the mountain have influenced his initial response in verse 19?

4. Why do you think Jesus asked the father the question he did in verse 21? (Consider the father's reply to Jesus as well.)

5. How did Jesus reply to the father's ambivalent hope that his son could be healed (verse 23)?

What does this say about the connection, if any, between belief and miracles?

6. Restate the father's response to Jesus in verse 24 in your own words. In what ways was this a true prayer?

7. If you wish, describe a time in your life when you found it difficult to believe and trust God completely to work. How was this difficulty reflected in your prayer life?

8. Try to visualize the dramatic scene described here as the boy is healed. Discuss the various feelings people might have had as this miracle of deliverance occurred. The father? People in the crowd? Jesus? The disciples?

9. How did the evil spirit react to Jesus (verses 20, 26)? Why?

10. What strikes you the most about this miracle of Jesus? Why?

What miraculous answers to prayer have you experienced or read about?

11. What concerns did the disciples' question in verse 28 suggest? What did Jesus' direct and simple answer reveal about Jesus' own ministry?

12. What are some steps you can take to make prayer a more consistent and confident part of your life?

How might prayer make you better able to fully trust God for "the impossible" during difficult times?

MIRACLES AND SPIRITUAL INSIGHT

John 9:1-41

Marie was a senior nursing student at Florida State University. She cared for a twelve-year-old boy named Kyle who had suffered from sickle cell anemia since the age of three. Complications caused a severe eye infection that required surgery. Afterwards the boy was told by his doctors, and other specialists verified, that he would never see again. Marie was a Christian, and though she was a bit afraid of offending the family, she decided to pray for Kyle.

"Kyle, do you ever pray?" He said no.

"Kyle, do you know about Jesus?" He answered yes.

"I am going to pray for you, but you need to believe that Jesus is going to help you get better." Then Marie held his hand and prayed for him only that one time. The next afternoon, when Marie was with him, Kyle began to identify colors and shapes.

Two days later the boy could see well enough to walk by himself. He was discharged from the hospital by awestruck doctors.*

I was a critical care nurse for eighteen years and now help sponsor the Nurses Christian Fellowship group at Florida State. I know Marie. This miracle caused no small stir in the nursing school and local hospital. How do you explain a miracle? The religious leaders in Jesus' day were challenged by a similar situation.

1. How do you respond to reports of a highly unusual miracle? Do you tend to be more skeptical or more accepting of such events? Why?

Read John 9:1-12.

◆ **2.** What question asked by the disciples led to the miracle described in this passage?

Why do you think the disciples asked this question?

*This story was documented in an article in The Journal of Christian Nursing (Winter, 1992), published by Nurses Christian Fellowship.

3. What points did Jesus emphasize in his reply?

What in Jesus' reply helps explain why Jesus initiated this miracle without the inquiry or invitation of the blind man?

4. Why do you think Jesus healed this man the way he did and not by verbal command alone?

5. Note the first place the man went after he received his sight. How did those who knew him respond to the miracle?

What made this man's story particularly difficult to believe?

Read John 9:13-34.

♦ **6.** How did the Pharisees investigate this miracle? Who did they question? What was their main concern?

7. What social and cultural pressures made the man's parents hesitant to acknowledge the miracle-worker, even when they had to acknowledge the miracle?

In what ways have you seen this same dynamic occur today?

8. Review the interrogation of the healed man (verses 17, 24-34). What emotions are evident in his dealings with the Pharisees?

What did the healed man conclude about Jesus?

◆ **9.** What final conclusion did the Pharisees make about the man born blind?

Considering that this man had heard this question all his life, how do you think he felt as he was excommunicated from the synagogue?

Read John 9:35-41.

10. Of what value would Jesus' actions and words be to the healed man at this particular time?

How did the man express his acknowledgment about who Jesus was?

11. What did Jesus' answer to the Pharisees' sneering question mean?

How did this reply address the basic concern behind the question asked at the beginning of the chapter (verse 2)?

12. Think back to your answer to question 1. How can this study help you to evaluate the reality of physical miracles?

13. Do you relate more with the blind man's belief or with the Pharisees' unbelief? Why? Ask God to show you ways to strengthen your spiritual insight.

MIRACLES AND SUFFERING

2 Corinthians 11:25-33; 12:1-10

From about my mid-twenties until my early forties, I suffered from a severe type of migraine headache. Every few weeks I would have a piercing pain on one side of my head that would last forty-eight to seventy-two hours. My head felt "heavy," I was extremely bothered by any kind of light, and no medication prevented or completely relieved the episodes. My sons remember how they helped "take care of Mama" by getting me a cold washcloth to lay over my eyes and how they tried to play "real quiet." My neurologist told me that migraine-type headaches tend to diminish when one got into their forties. But when you are twenty-something, a pastor's wife, registered nurse, and the mother of two toddlers, this is not great news.

I prayed that each headache would be the final one. Maybe the shorter episode I experienced about three weeks ago was the last one. Maybe not. I have learned in the last twenty-five years that God's grace really is sufficient, and that the absence of miracle does not mean an absence of mercy.

1. When has a time of pain or suffering in your life not been relieved even though you prayed for it?

Read 2 Corinthians 11:25-33.

♦ **2.** How did Paul describe the difficulties he faced as a servant of Christ?

What does Paul's experience indicate about the hardships of life even for faithful Christians?

3. What is the main point Paul expressed in this passage?

4. What kind of "weakness" did the story of Paul's escape illustrate?

How can dependence upon others affect our ability to trust God?

Read 2 Corinthians 12:1-10.

5. What extraordinary experience did Paul relate in verses 2-5?

Why do you think he chose to relate this experience in third person?

◆ **6.** What was Paul's attitude about his unrelieved "thorn in the flesh"?

How did he identify the source of his affliction?

7. What did Paul do in seeking relief from his malady? How did God help Paul?

◆ **8.** Why do you think Paul prayed about the problem only three times?

Do you think there are reasons to stop praying for physical healing today? Why or why not?

9. What is the role of Christ in manifesting God's power and grace in suffering?

10. Do you agree that Paul's attitude in verse 10 is possible only after prayer for healing has stopped? Why or why not?

11. Think of a situation involving physical disease or weakness from which you or someone you love still suffers. How is God's power being manifest in this weakness? How has God's grace been sufficient?

12. What does this study contribute to your understanding of how prayer, miracle, and faith relate to one another?

MIRACLES AND EVIL POWER

Mark 5:1-20

One of my first experiences with the powers of evil occurred when I was with a group of Christian college students at a weekend gathering in Berkeley, California. I vividly recall glimpses of a woman frantically running through the house, completely naked, smearing herself with some sort of oil, and shrieking in a voice I have never heard the likes of again. Mary, an older Christian woman who was with us, sent us to a room to pray. I didn't hesitate. We prayed for hours. The next morning we asked about the woman. Mary smiled and nodded to a beautiful young woman who sat there eating oatmeal with us. "I think you mean me," the woman said quietly. "But now I am new." It was a miracle.

We rejoiced in her healing and that she had come to trust in Jesus, but her demonic possession had been a frightening reality for us. Jesus encountered demon possession in people he met. But as we'll see from this story, when there's a showdown between evil powers, Jesus is the Lord who is in ultimate control.

1. When have you seen or experienced some sort of evil spiritual power? How did you respond?

Read Mark 5:1-14.

2. What was the setting of this miracle? Who was there?

◆ **3.** How is the demon-possessed man described (verses 1-5)? What characteristics of demonic possession in general can you gather from this description?

4. Note how the demons addressed Jesus. How might the fears the demon expressed in verse 7 have been related to this knowledge?

♦ **5.** Why do you think Jesus asked the question in verse 9?

♦ **6.** What desire did the demons express to Jesus?

How would you have felt if you had been one of those who tended the pigs?

Read Mark 5:15-20.

7. Contrast the man's behavior after his deliverance with his prior condition in verses 2-5 (his activity, state of mind, dress, and environment, etc.).

8. Considering the efforts made in the past by the townspeople to subdue the man (verse 4), why was their reaction surprising? What seemed to cause their greatest fear?

9. What was the newly healed man's desire (verse 18)? Suggest several reasons for his request.

10. What does Jesus' command to him show us about the purpose of some miracles?

What was the result of the man's obedience?

11. How has this study influenced your own attitude toward the reality of good and evil spiritual powers?

12. In what ways has Jesus' power and mercy transformed you or delivered you from evil in your life? How can you share what the Lord has done for you with someone else this week?

MIRACLES AND THE IMPOSSIBLE

John 11:17-44, 45-58; 12:17-19

Several years ago, just a few days before Christmas, my husband came home and told me that Tim, a high-schooler in our youth group, had just died of the leukemia he had fought for several years. As we cried together over this boy's death and grieved over so many "unanswered" prayers, our four-year-old, Robert, asked us what was wrong. We told him about Tim's illness and that he had died. And we told Robert about Tim's faith in Jesus: "Jesus has prepared a special place for him in his Father's big house."

At this news, Robert squealed with delight, clapped his hands, and ran in a circle around the living room. In our grief, we were surprised by this response. And then Robert said, "Tim is so lucky! He gets to see Jesus blow out all his candles!" We had always had a birthday cake for Jesus' birthday on Christmas, and four-year-olds love to blow out candles. Robert reminded us that God's ultimate miracle is his gift of eternal life. Jesus talked to Mary and Martha about this miraculous gift in response to their brother's death.

1. How does the promise of eternal life influence your attitude about miracles and earthly suffering?

Read John 11:17-44.

◆ **2.** What did Jesus discover when he arrived outside Bethany?

3. Why do you think Martha went to meet Jesus before his arrival at their home (verse 20)?

How did Martha's first words to Jesus reflect her feelings?

4. What did Martha mean by her confidence in Jesus (verse 22) in light of her conviction of the finality of her brother's death (verses 24, 39)?

5. What did Martha believe about the promise of Jesus in verse 23?

What distinction did Jesus make about her belief (verses 25-26)?

6. Compare Mary's first words to Jesus (verse 32) with those of Martha (verse 21). How might these reflect the conversations, feelings, and prayers of the two sisters during the illness of their brother?

7. How are the words "if only" reflected in your prayers and your attitude toward miracles?

8. How did Jesus respond to Mary's words and sorrow?

How do the various reactions people had to Jesus' arrival and his display of emotion reflect the way people today respond to death?

♦ **9.** What reason did Jesus give at Lazarus' tomb for his public prayer?

How did Jesus accomplish this miracle?

10. Earlier in Jesus' ministry in nearby Jerusalem, Jesus declared to skeptics, "For just as the Father raises the dead and gives them life, even so the Son gives life to whom he is pleased to give it." How did this miracle help people understand this declaration of Jesus?

Read John 11:45-48; 12:17-19.

◆ **11.** What impact did the raising of Lazarus have on Jesus' ministry?

How did various groups of people react to this extraordinary event?

12. How does your faith in Jesus' resurrection and in the resurrection of believers influence your confidence in "impossible" miracles happening today?

How does this same faith help you cope with disappointment when miracles do not happen?

MIRACLES AND WITNESS

Acts 3:1-10; 4:1-22

"Mary-by-Publix" is what people call her. She is old and blind. She stands outside the local Publix grocery story playing a small accordion and collecting donations in a box. Rain or shine, Mary-by-Publix greets you with, "A nice day, isn't it?" People are used to her presence, and if she's not there when the weather is cold, they miss her. What would the people in my hometown think if Mary miraculously received her sight one day? What would happen if a whole community had to suddenly deal with the miraculous power of God?

Jesus often healed people who were crippled and outcast. And he told his disciples that they would do greater works than he had done. The apostles Peter and John were available and eager to witness to the healing power of Jesus. But they may not have realized the division and commotion a miracle could cause in their local community, especially to someone everyone recognized.

1. Identify marginal or crippled people like Mary-by-Publix in your community. How might a miraculous change in their lives create an avenue for evangelism and witness?

Read Acts 3:1-10.

◆ **2.** What were Peter and John doing when they encountered the crippled man?

How do you usually view unexpected situations in your daily schedule? Why?

3. What had the crippled man's daily life been like (see Acts 4:22 also)?

4. How might a chronic, long-term condition such as this influence one's expectations of being healed?

5. What impresses you the most about how the beggar responded to his miraculous healing?

If you had been there and seen this man by the Gate Beautiful for years, what might you had thought about this miracle?

Read Acts 4:1-22.

6. Compare the effects of the crippled man's healing on the local people in the temple and on the local religious community. Why the different responses?

◆ **7.** What reasons did the Sadducees and other Jewish rulers have for putting Peter and John in jail (verses 2-4, 7, 16-17)?

8. Note the specific facts about Jesus that Peter highlighted in his response (verses 10-12). How did Peter's strategy help keep the focus on the work of Christ and not on the miracle-worker?

♦ **9.** How do you account for the apostles' boldness and their impact on the Sanhedrin (see verses 8, 13-14, 20-21)?

10. Do you relate more with the Sanhedrin's skeptical response to a miracle or to the people's believing joy? Why?

11. Skim these passages again. What were the ultimate outcomes and purposes of this miracle (see 3:6, 9-10; 4:9, 12, 16, 21-22)?

12. What have you "seen and heard" in your relationship with God that you can share with others?

MIRACLES AND SALVATION

Acts 7:54—8:3; 9:1-22

We've studied miracles of healing, miracles of nature, miracles of rescue and provision. But what about miracles of the soul, marked by inner changes in a person when he or she is forgiven of sin and follows Christ as Savior and Lord? C. S. Lewis writes in his biography, *Surprised By Joy,* that his conversion to Christianity was "like when a man, after long sleep, still lying motionless in bed, becomes aware that he is now awake." The early church bishop, Augustine of Hippo, described his experience of belief as "a peaceful light streaming into my heart, all the dark shadows of doubt fled away."

This stepping "out of darkness and into [God's] wonderful light" (1 Peter 2:9) is the greatest of miracles and is available to everyone. Believers experience this conversion differently; some are dramatic, some are not. Whether an eight-year-old whose heart is opened to the truth by a Bible story, a rebellious teenager who realizes God's unconditional love, or a college professor who surrenders to Christ as the ultimate Truth, what God offers us in Christ is a gift. The apostle Paul wrote, "For it is by grace you have been saved, through faith—and this not from yourselves, it is the gift of God—not by works, so that no one can boast" (Ephesians 2:8-9). Paul should know. The change it made in his life was truly miraculous.

1. What miraculous stories of conversion have you read or heard about recently?

Read Acts 7:54—8:3 and Acts 9:1-9.

♦ **2.** What role did Saul, an up-and-coming Jewish Pharisee, play in the stoning of Stephen?

♦ **3.** Why do you think Saul hated those of "the Way" who claimed Jesus was the Messiah (look for clues in 7:54-57; 9:2)?

4. What dramatic events marked Paul's encounter with Jesus?

How well did the other men comprehend what had happened?

5. Why do you think Paul responded as he did to Jesus' miraculous intervention?

What might he have been thinking or praying about for three days?

Read Acts 9:10-22.

6. What was Ananias's first response to God's command?

Have you ever doubted the work of God in someone else's life? Why?

7. Why do you think the Lord revealed his plans for Saul (verses 15-16)?

8. How does Ananias identify the reasons he was sent to Saul (verse 17)?

How does Saul's response reflect God's miraculous work?

9. Compare the Saul in verses 18-22 with the Saul in chapters 8:3 and 9:1-2. What changes are evident?

10. How did people respond to Paul's sudden and complete change?

What about Saul's life was miraculous proof that Jesus is truly the Christ?

11. Think about your own experience of salvation. If there is time and you are comfortable doing so, tell your story. Why is the forgiveness and grace of Christ *the* greatest miracle in your life?

What changes is the Holy Spirit making in your life?

LEADER'S NOTES

■ **Study 1/Miracles and the Miracle Worker**

Question 6. Moses believed that the people were ready to throw rocks at him and kill him (Exodus 17:4), and God told him, essentially, to risk being a good target "in front of the people"! Obeying God at times of real personal risk can create the circumstances for God's miraculous provision or intervention.

Question 8. No date is given, but the Israelites probably arrived at Kadesh near the end of their forty years of wandering in the wilderness. Their recent history had been full of God's miraculous provision (the deliverance from slavery in Egypt, and manna for food), which makes their unbelief even more trying to Moses.

Question 9. Moses' language in Numbers 20:10 is strikingly harsh, calling the people "rebels." Moses also seemed to credit the miraculous power to himself when he said, "must *we* bring you water . . ." No longer fearing the people, he also seemed to have lost his fear of the Lord. No longer dependent on God for protection, he credits himself for provision.

Question 11. Not only had Moses lost much of his love for God's people, but he had forgotten much of his reverence for God's holiness. Moses once took his shoes off when Yahweh came to him in the burning bush. Moses understood then that he was on "holy ground" (see Exodus 3). It now seems that Moses, no longer awestruck by the God he met on the mountain, takes matters into his own hands, strikes the rock in anger and pride, and disobeys.

■ Study 2/Miracles and Obedience

Question 2. Jonah was a prophet in Israel during c. 785-760 B.C., at a time when Assyria was Israel's greatest enemy. Nineveh was the large capitol city of the Assyrian empire, about 500 miles northeast of Israel. Jonah headed west, first to Joppa on the western coast of Israel, and then to Tarshish, a western Phoenician port thought by many to be located on the southwest coast of Spain.

Question 3. Jonah's withdrawal, resignation, and prolonged sleep may indicate the depth of Jonah's depression in the midst of his refusal to obey God. When his faith was challenged by unbelievers, feelings of guilt may have compounded Jonah's dilemma.

Question 12. Some scholars think that the number of people mentioned here is metaphorical. Others have suggested that the 120,000 people of Nineveh who did not know "their right hand from their left" represented the approximate number of innocent children in that great city. Either way, God's compassion was great, and even extended to all creation ("cattle," verse 11), not just people.

◼ Study 3/Miracles and Faithfulness

Question 2. In the 6th century B.C., the Babylonian empire conquered the Jewish nation of Judah. The best, young Jewish leaders were exiled and educated in Babylonian culture. Even the new names given to the four Jewish men incorporated the names of various Babylonian gods.

Question 3. Some of the royal food and wine would have been considered unclean for Jewish believers, because portions would have violated their Levitical dietary laws, been offered to idols, or poured on pagan altars.

◼ Study 4/Miracles and Power

Question 2. The Greek word for "miraculous signs" used in John 6:2 indicates an extraordinary phenomenon by which anything is known or distinguished. There is a sense in which a "sign" does not exist for itself, but serves to point to a greater destination or purpose.

Question 5. Human nature being what it is, any remnants of the miraculously multiplied bread could easily have become good-luck charms or magical religious relics. Perhaps Jesus was trying to control any potential misuse of his miracles.

It's also interesting that there is no mention of any fish left over. Fish would quickly spoil, and the omission of this particular detail is a good "eyewitness tag," reflecting an eyewitness account to the miraculous nature of the event itself.

Question 6. At the beginning of his ministry, Jesus had been tempted in the wilderness by Satan to use miraculous power for personal gain (see Matthew 4:1-11 and Luke 4:1-13). Jesus could have easily used this or any other miracle to his advantage as well, if his purpose had been to build a worldly kingdom. He avoided this temptation by keeping his good purposes in view and refusing to capitalize on weaknesses of people.

Question 8. The people are associating Jesus' miracle with the time when manna had been miraculously provided for the Israelites in the wilderness for forty years! This knowledge of "free food" in the past certainly intensified the interest of the people in seeking this sign from Jesus.

■ Study 5/Miracles and Mercy

Question 1. The distinction between *grace* and *mercy* can be summarized in this way: Grace gives us what we don't deserve; mercy does not give us what we do deserve. God's grace gives us eternal life. God's mercy spares us his wrath.

Question 7. It is wise to consider Jesus' confidence in the light of Peter's enthusiasm. Jesus encouraged Peter's experiment in faith. God isn't nervous about our risks and/or "failures" as we often are, but wants us to not be afraid to risk and learn and trust.

■ Study 6/Miracles and Prayer

Question 3. Jesus' transfiguration in Mark 9:1-8 was a brief revelation of his deity and an affirmation by God the Father of his ministry. Peter, James, and John were witnesses to this extraordinary event. The reminder of his place in glory, as well as the situation he was now facing, could have created a weariness and longing for "home" in Jesus. We can be sure that this response of Jesus was not sinful.

■ Study 7/Miracles and Spiritual Insight

Question 2. The problem of congenital birth defects has long been a focus of theological discussion. In Jesus' day rabbinical schools often differed on how to answer difficult questions. It was common for the students of a certain rabbi to ask the opinion of their teacher. The options expressed by the disciples here reflected the prominent views held by various rabbinical schools of that time.

Question 6. The Pharisees were one of the dominant religious groups during Jesus' day. They were known for their strict adherence to Jewish traditions and religious law. They also believed that the Messiah would come. The healing of congenital blindness had been promised in the Old Testament as a clear evidence of the Messiah. (See Isaiah 35:5 and 42:7.) To acknowledge this man's healing held significant religious implications for these Jewish leaders. The healing of a person born blind had never happened before! In addition, they were very annoyed that Jesus disregarded the law by healing—"working"—on the Sabbath.

Question 9. The local community synagogue was the religious and political stronghold of the Pharisees. The very thing the parents of the healed man feared (in John 9:22-23) was inflicted on their son. The healed man became—again—socially, economically, and religiously, an outcast.

■ Study 8/Miracles and Suffering

Question 2. Paul is talking here to the church in Corinth. One problem in the church here was a belief that material blessing was a sign of God's favor and that suffering always indicated personal sin. Paul's litany of hardship was intended to refute that false teaching.

Question 6. We do not know for sure what Paul's thorn in the flesh was. Some believe it may have been epilepsy or an eye problem. Whatever it was, it was chronic and debilitating. We live in a world affected by sin, and are not shielded from disease, suffering, or death. Though God is not the cause of suffering, he can use the suffering we experience from living in a fallen world for his own purposes. He is the final Overcomer of suffering.

Question 8. There is no way to be certain why Paul limited his request for healing, but the discussion of the group should be helpful in identifying attitudes held about suffering, prayer, and coping with hardship and personal weakness.

■ Study 9/Miracles and Evil Power

Question 3. The self-destructive tendencies of the demon-possessed man can be a general characteristic of demonic power. The evil one seeks to deface and destroy people created in the image of God.

Question 5. A couple of explanations have been suggested for why Jesus asked for the evil spirit's name. "First, the ancient belief that knowledge of the name gave power over an adversary. Alternatively, and more probably, it was to recall the man to a sense of his own personality apart from the demon. *Legion* was a Latin word, suggesting numbers, strength, and oppression" *(The New Bible Commentary: Revised,* p. 862. Grand Rapids, Mich.: Eerdmans, 1970).

Question 6. The demons were terrified of being sent "out of the area." Luke 8:31 states that they were afraid of going "into the Abyss" perhaps suggesting that the spirits feared complete disembodiment (taken from *The New Bible Commentary: Revised,* p. 862).

■ Study 10/Miracles and the Impossible

Question 2. There is evidence of an early Jewish belief that for the first three days after death, the soul of the dead person lingered near the body. The first three days of mourning were particularly intense because it was believed the dead person could witness the grief of family and friends. The mention of "four days" in John 11:17 creates the climate for an "impossible" miracle.

Question 9. You may want to compare the means Jesus used for this miracle with the creative means of God revealed in Genesis 1 and John 1:1-5. Only God can create something from nothing; only God can bring life from death.

Question 11. John 12:17 contains the only reference in Scripture to Lazarus after he was raised from the dead. It does not appear, in the biblical account, that Lazarus had any lasting notoriety.

■ Study 11/Miracles and Witness

Question 2. "The Jews observed prayer three times a day—morning (9:00), afternoon (3:00), and evening, . . . when devout Jews often went to the temple to pray" *(Life Application Bible,* p. 1948. Wheaton, Ill.: Tyndale House, 1988, 1989, 1990, 1991). It's likely that Peter and John had seen this man, among others, often as they entered the temple courts. Perhaps this familiarity was one of the reasons they responded so quickly. They showed compassion and faith with their willingness to put their prayer meeting on hold in order to make a difference and witness for Christ.

Question 7. The Sadducees were a Jewish religious party that did not affirm the belief in the resurrection of the dead, so the apostles' emphasis on Jesus' resurrection was particularly heretical to them. At the time of the arrest there is no mention made of the crippled man's miraculous healing, though this miraculous show of power and the apostles' subsequent popularity seemed to be their main concern.

Question 9. The Sanhedrin was the same council of Jewish rulers and elders which had tried Jesus and condemned him to death. They thought they were done with him!

■ Study 12/Miracles and Salvation

Question 2. "Saul" was Paul's Hebrew name. (See Acts 13:9.) "Born . . . the son of a Pharisee, Saul was cradled in orthodox Judaism . . . and was a superior, zealous rabbinical student. . . . At his first appearance in Acts, probably at least 30 years old, he was already an acknowledged leader in Judaism" *(The Zondervan Pictorial Bible Dictionary*, Merrill C. Tenney, ed., p. 627. Grand Rapids, Mich.: 1967). Stoning was the usual form of punishment for blasphemy, according to Hebrew law (see Leviticus 24:16).

Question 3. Paul was convinced that he "ought to do all that was possible to oppose the name of Jesus of Nazareth" (Acts 26:9), and that by so doing he was vindicating the true God. Their heresy was evident in Stephen's claims (Acts 7:54-56), and they were dangerous influences on others in the synagogues (Acts 9:2).

WHAT SHOULD WE STUDY NEXT?

To help your group answer that question, we've listed the Fisherman Guides by category so you can choose your next study.

TOPICAL STUDIES

Becoming Women of Purpose, Barton

Building Your House on the Lord, Brestin

Discipleship, Reapsome

Doing Justice, Showing Mercy, Wright

Encouraging Others, Johnson

Examining the Claims of Jesus, Brestin

Friendship, Brestin

The Fruit of the Spirit, Briscoe

Great Doctrines of the Bible, Board

Great Passages of the Bible, Plueddemann

Great People of the Bible, Plueddemann

Great Prayers of the Bible, Plueddemann

Growing Through Life's Challenges, Reapsome

Guidance & God's Will, Stark

Higher Ground, Brestin

How Should a Christian Live? (1,2, & 3 John), Brestin

Marriage, Stevens

Moneywise, Larsen

One Body, One Spirit, Larsen

The Parables of Jesus, Hunt

Prayer, Jones

The Prophets, Wright

Proverbs & Parables, Brestin

Relationships, Hunt

Satisfying Work, Stevens & Schoberg

Senior Saints, Reapsome

Sermon on the Mount, Hunt

The Ten Commandments, Briscoe

When Servants Suffer, Rhodes

Who Is Jesus? Van Reken

Worship, Sibley

BIBLE BOOK STUDIES

Genesis, Fromer & Keyes

Job, Klug

Psalms, Klug

Proverbs: Wisdom That Works, Wright

Ecclesiastes, Brestin

Jonah, Habakkuk, & Malachi, Fromer & Keyes

Matthew, Sibley

Mark, Christensen

Luke, Keyes

John: Living Word, Kuniholm

Acts 1-12, Christensen

Paul (Acts 13-28), Christensen

Romans: The Christian Story, Reapsome

1 Corinthians, Hummel

Strengthened to Serve (2 Corinthians), Plueddemann

Galatians, Titus & Philemon, Kuniholm

Ephesians, Baylis

Philippians, Klug

Colossians, Shaw

Letters to the Thessalonians, Fromer & Keyes

Letters to Timothy, Fromer & Keyes

Hebrews, Hunt

James, Christensen

1 & 2 Peter, Jude, Brestin

How Should a Christian Live? (1, 2 & 3 John), Brestin

Revelation, Hunt

BIBLE CHARACTER STUDIES

Ruth & Daniel, Stokes

David: Man after God's Own Heart, Castleman

Job, Klug

King David: Trusting God for a Lifetime, Castleman

Elijah, Castleman

Men Like Us, Heidebrecht & Scheuermann

Peter, Castleman

Paul (Acts 13-28), Christensen

Great People of the Bible, Plueddemann

Women Like Us, Barton

Women Who Achieved for God, Christensen

Women Who Believed God, Christensen